T0365864

My Dad is in Jail... I Won't Fail

Written by
M.A. Rodriguez

Illustrated by
Joel Ray Pellerin

Order this book online at www.trafford.com
or email orders@trafford.com

Most Trafford titles are also available at major online book retailers.

Printed in the United States of America.

ISBN: 978-1-4907-2050-0 (sc)
978-1-4907-2049-4 (e)

Library of Congress Control Number: 2013922676

Trafford rev. 12/16/2013

Trafford
PUBLISHING® www.trafford.com
North America & international
toll-free: 1 888 232 4444 (USA & Canada)
fax: 812 355 4082

Dedicated to the love of my life
Mila.

I love my daddy!

He always reads books to me.

This is my favorite thing of all.

He knows it makes me happy.

I came home, but my daddy was not there.

Mom said Daddy did something wrong,

and he had to go.

I was so sad that day;

I did not even want to play.

Dad sends pictures for me to color and talks

to me on the phone.

He says, "Don't ever feel bad

'cause I have done wrong."

I love hearing his voice on the phone.

Families change.

This is quite clear.

My daddy is not here,

but Mom, Poppy, and Granny

always make me cheer.

My Poppy says when a person

goes to jail, they have to think about

what they have done, like a time-out.

I know that is not very much fun!

Granny tells me sometimes I might feel

angry or sad.

She draws with me,

and I feel better sending it to my dad.

I worry about what the kids might think.

They might make fun of me

and cause a "big stink."

But then I just show them

I am me and give them a big old wink.

I just have to try to remember

how much I am loved by my friends and

family and even angels from above.

Printed in the United States
by Baker & Taylor Publisher Services